All About MONEY

Spending Money

Ben Hubbard
and Beatriz Castro

CRABTREE
PUBLISHING COMPANY
WWW.CRABTREEBOOKS.COM

CRABTREE
PUBLISHING COMPANY
WWW.CRABTREEBOOKS.COM

Author: Ben Hubbard

Editorial director: Kathy Middleton

Editors: Julia Bird

Proofreader: Ellen Rodger

Illustrator: Beatriz Castro

Prepress technician: Ken Wright

Print coordinator: Katherine Berti

Every attempt has been made to clear copyright. Should there be any inadvertent omission please apply to the publisher for rectification.

The website addresses (URLs) included in this book were valid at the time of going to press. However, it is possible that contents or addresses may have changed since the publication of this book. No responsibility for any such changes can be accepted by either the author or the Publisher.

Library and Archives Canada Cataloguing in Publication

Title: Spending money / Ben Hubbard and [illustrated by] Beatriz Castro.
Names: Hubbard, Ben, 1973- author. | Castro, Beatriz (Castro Arbaizar), illustrator.
Description: Series statement: All about money | Previously published: London: Franklin Watts, 2019. | Includes index.
Identifiers: Canadiana (print) 20190195355 | Canadiana (ebook) 20190195363 | ISBN 9780778773733 (hardcover) | ISBN 9780778773849 (softcover) | ISBN 9781427124999 (HTML)
Subjects: LCSH: Finance, Personal—Juvenile literature. | LCSH: Consumption (Economics)—Juvenile literature. | LCSH: Money—Juvenile literature.
Classification: LCC HG179 .H833 2020 | DDC j332.024—dc23

Library of Congress Cataloging-in-Publication Data

Names: Hubbard, Ben, 1973- author. | Castro, Beatriz (Castro Arbaizar), illustrator.
Title: Spending money / Ben Hubbard and ; Beatriz Castro.
Description: New York, New York : Crabtree Publishing Company, [2019] | Series: All about money | Includes index.
Identifiers: LCCN 2019043658 (print) | LCCN 2019043659 (ebook) | ISBN 9780778773733 (hardcover) | ISBN 9780778773849 (paperback) | ISBN 9781427124999 (ebook)
Subjects: LCSH: Money--Juvenile literature. | Shopping--Juvenile literature. | Basic needs--Juvenile literature.
Classification: LCC HG221.5 .H825 2019 (print) | LCC HG221.5 (ebook) | DDC 640.73--dc23
LC record available at https://lccn.loc.gov/2019043658
LC ebook record available at https://lccn.loc.gov/2019043659

Crabtree Publishing Company

www.crabtreebooks.com   1–800–387–7650
Published by Crabtree Publishing Company in 2020

First published in Great Britain in 2019 by The Watts Publishing Group
Copyright ©The Watts Publishing Group, 2019

Printed in the U.S.A./012020/CG20191115

Published in Canada
Crabtree Publishing
616 Welland Ave.
St. Catharines, Ontario
L2M 5V6

Published in the United States
Crabtree Publishing
PMB 59051
350 Fifth Avenue, 59th Floor
New York, New York 10118

Spending Money

This book is all about money. Why is money important? You can't eat or drink it, but most of us need money to survive. We use money to pay for nearly everything we want or need, including clothing, electricity, food, and water. It is hard to imagine a world without money.

Some people say money makes the world go around.

When we have some money, we have to make choices. What should we do with our money? We can:

Save it

Spend it

Share it

Or, make more money!

In the following pages, Ava wonders how to spend her money. Keep reading to see what she buys!

After her grandfather died, Ava **inherited** some money.
Her parents put most of it into a **savings account**.
But they also gave Ava some money to spend.

Ava and her mom go shopping. A lot of things are **on sale**, which means they are being sold cheaper than usual. There is so much to choose from that it makes Ava's head spin!

There are great **discounts** on some sparkly shoes. Ava loves the way they look, but she already has a pair she likes.

Ava and her mom come back from the store without the sneakers. Ava still has all of her money. At home, Ava's dad is shopping for work shirts **online**.

Stores drive me crazy! It's calmer online and I can take my time.

And bones...

Look, there are online stores for kids' clothes, too.

One online store has the same
sneakers Ava saw in town.
They are even cheaper online.

Look Mom, the shoes are
cheaper here. I'm glad
I didn't buy them
at the store.

It always pays to shop
around for the best price.

Ava is really tempted to buy the sneakers online. It's such a big discount. She asks her dad for his advice.

Sometimes online stores are not what they seem. Prices may change at **checkout** or the website might sell fake products. You have to be careful.

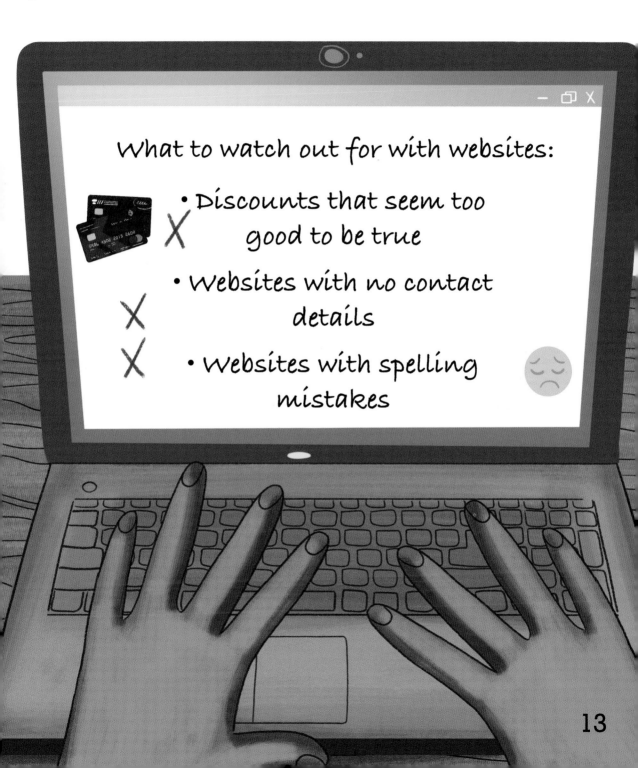

What to watch out for with websites:

X • Discounts that seem too good to be true

X • Websites with no contact details

X • Websites with spelling mistakes

Ava doesn't know what to do. Should she buy the online sneakers, even if the discount isn't as good as she thought? She asks her older brother's advice.

Ava realizes her brother has a point. She got so caught up with getting the best deal that she forgot whether she actually wanted the sneakers.

You're right! Why have I been wasting my time thinking about those shoes?

It's easy to do. But just because something is discounted doesn't mean it's worth buying.

15

Ava didn't realize spending money could be so complicated! To help, her mom suggests Ava write a list of some things she actually needs. That way, she can make a good decision about how to spend her money.

Have you heard the expression "that money is burning a hole in your pocket"?

It means feeling like you have to spend your money right now.

At school, Ava shows her friends her lists of "needs" and "wants." But one friend disagrees. He is an **immigrant** from a country where there is a war. He says Ava doesn't really "need" anything more than she already has.

Where I come from, many people need food and shelter because they don't have them.

Oh! I didn't know that.

After talking to her friends, Ava throws away her "wants" list. Together, she and her friends write a new "needs" list.

On the way home from school, Ava tells her brother how lucky they are. Their parents provide them with everything they need, and they don't have to worry about money.

Ava says she still doesn't know what to buy.
The things she wrote on her "wants" list don't
seem so important anymore.

That weekend, Ava's parents take her to a local art store which is having a sale. Ava is amazed by all the beautiful colored pencils, paints, and paper. This is what she wants!

Look at these lovely pencils and pads for sketching!

After she picks some pencils and paper, Ava counts out her money and gives it to the store owner. She has finally spent some of her money!

It's nice to support small stores in our area.

Thank you. These days, a lot of people shop online at big department stores instead of coming into local businesses.

Ava has finally bought herself something useful, which may also help her in the future.

Ava soon has some art to show her parents.

Ta-daa!

That's great. I'm so glad you bought art supplies instead of sneakers.

Yes, good artwork and memories last forever.

Ava stays busy with her art for weeks. She even forgets that she still has some money left to spend. Then one day....

Oh, look!

What will you spend it on Ava?

What will she spend
her money on?
Ava wonders…

In the end, Ava decides to make some other people happy with the rest of her money. She spends it on treats to share with her friends.

There was even a little
bit of money left over for
a final treat…

Quiz

Now that you've reached the end of the book, how much do you think you've learned about spending money? Take this test to find out.

1

What is a discounted item?
- **a** One that is cheaper than normal
- **b** One that is more expensive that normal
- **c** One that is out-of-date

2

Where do people often buy things?
- **a** Onlion
- **b** Ontime
- **c** Online

3

What *don't* people need to survive?
- **a** Water
- **b** Food
- **c** Fancy sneakers

4

Where do people often keep their money?
- **a** A bank savings account
- **b** A wall savings account
- **c** A hill savings account

5

What do you sometimes have to pay at online stores?
- **a** picking
- **b** plotting
- **c** shipping

Answers
1.a, 2.c, 3.c, 4.a, 5.c

Money words

checkout
The point at which you pay for something you are buying

discount
A reduction in the usual price of something

immigrant
Someone who has come to live in a new country from another country

inherit
When you receive money or items that were left to you by someone who has died

on sale
When things are sold at a reduced price

online
On the Internet

savings account
A bank account that adds money, called interest, to the money you have in the account

Money facts

There's always more to learn about money.
Check out these facts!

- Most people spend over 75,000 hours of their lives working to earn money.

- An ATM (Automated Teller Machine) is where people can withdraw cash from their bank account using a card. The first one was used in London, England, in 1967.

- Many countries have laws against defacing paper money. This means damaging the bills by drawing or writing on them.

- Some companies raise money by selling shares to people. This means the people get a share of the company's profits.

- Ancient Roman soldiers were paid in salt. The word salary comes from the Latin word salarium, for salt money.